CONTINENTS

South America

Mary Virginia Fox

Heinemann
LIBRARY

www.heinemann.co.uk/library
Visit our website to find out more information about Heinemann Library books.

To order:

☎ Phone ++44 (0)1865 888066

📄 Send a fax to ++44 (0)1865 314091

💻 Visit the Heinemann Bookshop at www.heinemann.co.uk/library to browse our catalogue and order online.

First published in Great Britain by Heinemann Library, Halley Court, Jordan Hill, Oxford OX2 8EJ, a division of Reed Educational and Professional Publishing Ltd. Heinemann is a registered trademark of Reed Educational and Professional Publishing Ltd.

OXFORD MELBOURNE AUCKLAND JOHANNESBURG BLANTYRE GABORONE IBADAN PORTSMOUTH NH (USA) CHICAGO

Designed by Depke Design
Originated by Dot Gradations
Printed by South China Printing in Hong Kong, China

06 05 04 03 02
10 9 8 7 6 5 4 3 2 1
ISBN 0 431 15793 6

British Library Cataloguing in Publication Data
Fox, Mary Virginia
    South America. – (Continents)
    1.South America – Juvenile literature
    I.Title
    918

Acknowledgements
The publishers are grateful to the following for permission to reproduce copyright material: Earth Scenes/Fabio Colonbini, p. 5; Photo Edit/E. Zuckerman, p. 6; Earth Scenes/Breck P. Kent, pp. 9, 19; Tony Stone/Kevin Schafer, p. 11; Corbis/Adam Woolfitt, p. 13; Brian Vikander, p. 14; Animals Animals/Partridge, p. 15; Earth Scenes, p. 16; Tony Stone/Avenida Paulista, p. 20; DDB Stock Photo/ Robert Fried, p. 21; Peter Arnold/Jeff Greenberg, Inc., p. 23; Earth Scenes/Nigel J. H. Smith, p. 24; Earth Scenes/Michael Fogden, p. 25; Bruce Coleman/Timothy O'Keefe, Inc., p. 26; Tony Stone/Ary Diesendruck, p. 27; Photo Researchers/Georg Gerster, p. 28.

Cover photo reproduced with permission of Science Photo Library/Tom Van Sant, Geosphere Project/Planetary Visions.

Our thanks to Jane Bingham for her assistance in the preparation of this book.

Every effort has been made to contact copyright holders of any material reproduced in this book. Any omissions will be rectified in subsequent printings if notice is given to the Publisher.

Contents

Some words are shown in bold, **like this**.
You can find out what they mean by looking in the glossary.

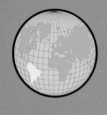

Where is South America?

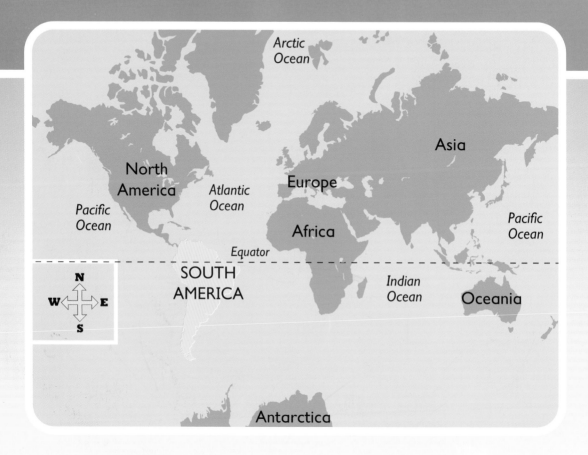

Arctic Ocean

Asia

North America

Atlantic Ocean

Europe

Pacific Ocean

Africa

Pacific Ocean

Equator

SOUTH AMERICA

Indian Ocean

Oceania

N
W E
S

Antarctica

A continent is a vast mass of land that covers part of the Earth's surface. There are seven continents in the world, and South America is the fourth largest. South America is joined to the continent of North America by a narrow strip of land. Most of South America lies below the **equator**.

Sandy beach on Brazil's Atlantic coast

South America lies between two great oceans – the Pacific Ocean to the west and the Atlantic Ocean to the east. To the north of South America is the Caribbean Sea. At the southern tip of South America the coast is very rocky. In Brazil, on the eastern side of the continent, there are long, sandy beaches.

Weather

Amazon River winding through the rainforest

The **equator** crosses South America near its widest part. Around the equator is the world's largest **rainforest**. In the rainforest, the weather is **tropical** – hot and rainy all year round. To the north and south of the rainforest are areas of grassland, known as *llanos*. Here, it is hot and mainly dry.

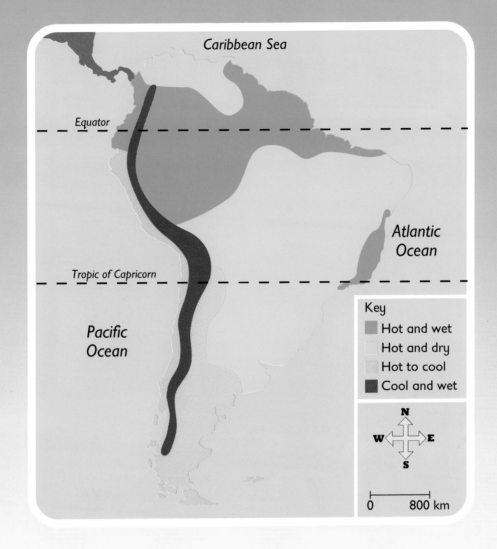

In the high Andes Mountains, on the western side of South America, the weather is cool and rainy. At the continent's southern tip it is very cold and windy. This southern part of South America is closest to the continent of Antarctica, which is the coldest area on Earth.

Mountains and deserts

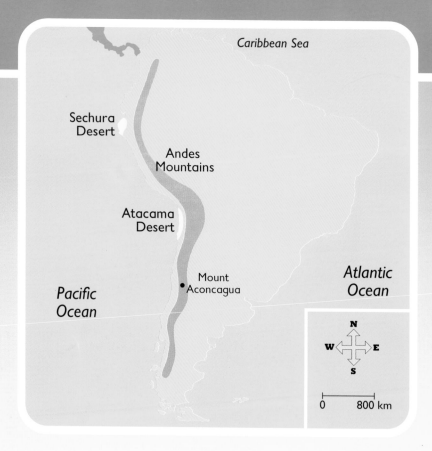

The snow-capped Andes Mountains are the longest mountain **range** in the world, stretching for 8900 kilometres. The tallest peak is Mount Aconcagua in Argentina. There are hundreds of **volcanoes** in the Andes, and some are still **erupting**. People **mine** for gold, silver and copper in the Andes.

The rocky Atacama Desert in Peru

Along the west coast of South America are stretches of stony desert. These deserts are sheltered from the rain by the Andes Mountains. In parts of the Atacama Desert, no rain has ever been recorded. During the day, the temperature in these deserts can reach 50 °C, but at night it is bitterly cold.

Rivers

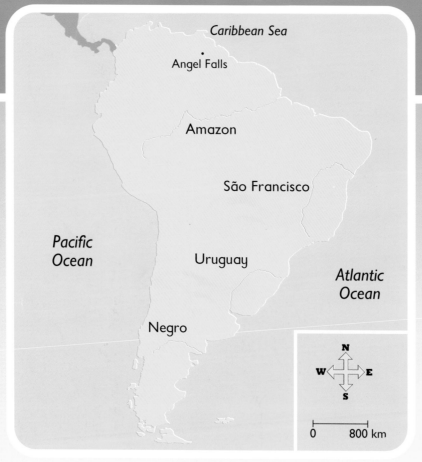

More water flows through the Amazon River than through any other river in the world. Its **source** is an icy lake in the Andes Mountains, and its **mouth** is on the Atlantic coast of Brazil. The Amazon flows for 6400 kilometres. For most of its journey, it winds through dense **rainforest**.

Angel Falls, Venezuela

The Angel River drops for nearly one kilometre into a deep **gorge** in northeastern South America. This is Angel Falls, the tallest waterfall in the world. In some parts of South America, people use energy from fast-moving rivers to create electricity. This kind of power is called hydroelectricity.

Lakes

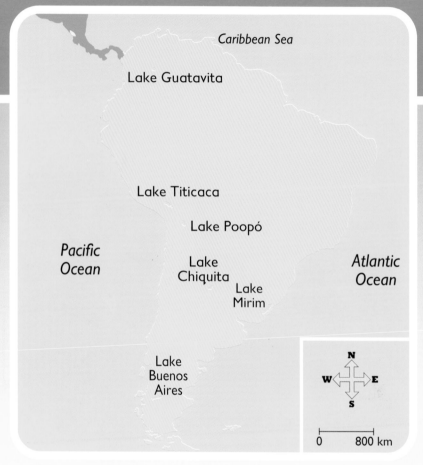

Caribbean Sea

Lake Guatavita

Lake Titicaca

Lake Poopó

Pacific
Ocean

Lake
Chiquita

Lake
Mirim

Atlantic
Ocean

Lake
Buenos
Aires

N
W E
S

0   800 km

Lake Titicaca is high in the Andes Mountains. It is so large
that it warms the air around it. Giant frogs live among the
reeds at the edge of the lake. The local people make boats
from the reeds and use these boats to go fishing on the lake.

Lake Guatavita, Colombia

Lake Guatavita is a circular lake in the northern Andes. Hundreds of years ago, the people who lived in the Andes believed that this was the place where the sun was born. Before a new ruler was crowned, he had to sail out to the centre of the lake and throw golden gifts into the water for the gods.

Animals

Alpacas in Peru carrying grass

High in the mountains, farmers keep llamas, vicuñas and alpacas. These strong animals look like small camels. They provide milk, meat and long, fine wool, which the mountain people weave into clothes. Their **dung** can be burnt as fuel, and they are very good at carrying heavy loads.

Anaconda searching for prey

The **rainforests** of South America are home to thousands of creatures. Parrots perch in the trees, monkeys swing from branches, and huge anacondas wait in rivers to pounce on their prey. Anacondas are one of the world's largest snakes. They can open their jaws wide enough to eat a whole goat.

Plants

Sap from a rubber tree

Hundreds of products come from the trees and plants of South America. Rubber is made from the **sap** of rubber trees. The sapodilla tree produces a substance called chicle, which is used to make chewing gum. Quinine, a drug that is used to fight **malaria**, comes from the cinchona tree.

Cacao trees in Brazil

Chocolate is made from cocoa which comes from the seeds of the cacao tree. The people of South America were among the first people in the world to make chocolate. Cacao trees grow wild in the **rainforests**, but today cacao is often grown on farms. Farmers **export** cocoa to countries all over the world.

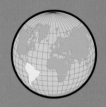

Languages

Caribbean Sea
Guyana
Venezuela
Suriname
Columbia
French Guiana
Ecuador
Brazil
Peru
Bolivia
Pacific Ocean
Paraguay
Atlantic Ocean
Uruguay
Chile
Argentina

N
W E
S

0   800 km

There are thirteen countries in South America. Most people in these countries speak Spanish or Portuguese. Around 500 years ago, explorers from Spain and Portugal arrived in South America and began to settle there. Many Portuguese **settlers** lived in Brazil. The Spanish people settled mainly in the west of South America.

Yahua people from Peru

The first people to live in South America were **Native Americans**. They had their own languages and **traditions**. Some groups of Native Americans, such as the Yahua people from the mountains of Peru and the Yanomani people from the **rainforests** of Brazil, still speak the language of their **ancestors**.

Cities

São Paulo, Brazil

São Paulo is a busy port on the southeast coast. It is the largest city in South America, and a centre for buying and selling coffee. São Paulo also has many factories. Steel, chemicals, televisions and computers are all produced in or near the city.

Santiago, Chile

The city of Santiago was built by Spanish **settlers** at the base of the Andes Mountains. Money made from **mining** silver and copper turned Santiago into a wealthy city. Santiago is the capital of Chile. It has many beautiful, broad streets and a fine, Spanish-style cathedral.

Quito, Ecuador

Quito is one of the highest cities in the world. It sits on the side of a **volcano**. It is the **capital** of Ecuador and one of the oldest cities in South America. Five hundred years ago, it was the capital of the ancient kingdom of Quito, which was ruled by the Inca people.

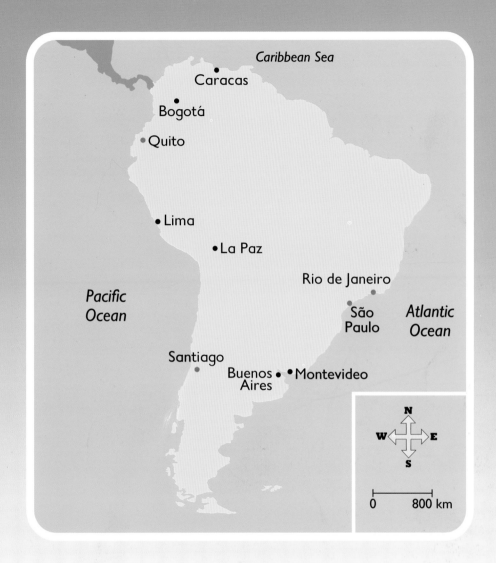

This map shows the main cities of South America. Caracas, Bogotá, Quito, Lima, La Paz, Santiago, Montevideo and Buenos Aires are all **capital cities**. Rio de Janeiro, in Brazil, is the busiest port in South America. Rio is famous for its beautiful beaches and its lively **festivals**.

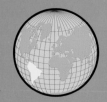 # In the country

Houses on stilts by the Amazon River

In the **rainforests** of South America, most people live on rivers. Travelling by boat is the easiest way to get from one village to another. Today, the way of life of the rainforest people is in danger. Many trees are being cut down for **timber** and large areas of forest are being cleared to create farming land.

House built from clay, Peru

High in the mountains, sheep and llama **herders** live in small houses with thick, clay walls to keep out the cold. In the **humid** lands around the rainforest, farmers grow coffee, cacao and sugar beet. In the cooler grasslands of the south, people grow wheat and there are huge cattle ranches.

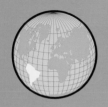

Famous places

Machu Picchu, Peru

Over 500 years ago, the Inca people of the Andes built a walled city called Machu Picchu. The city contained houses, palaces and temples. There was also an **observatory**, where people could study the stars. Machu Picchu stayed hidden from the rest of the world for hundreds of years.

Rio de Janeiro, Brazil

In Rio de Janeiro, a giant statue of Jesus looks down on the harbour. The statue is 30 metres tall. It can be seen from miles away and at night it is lit up. Many people in South America are Christians. The Spanish and Portuguese **settlers** built churches and cathedrals all over the continent.

Church carved from a salt mine in Colombia

Many people work in **mines** in South America. In Chile, miners dig up copper, and in Peru they mine for silver. Gold, emerald and salt are all mined in Colombia. The country has a famous Gold Museum and a church made from a salt mine. Even the statues in the church are carved from salt.

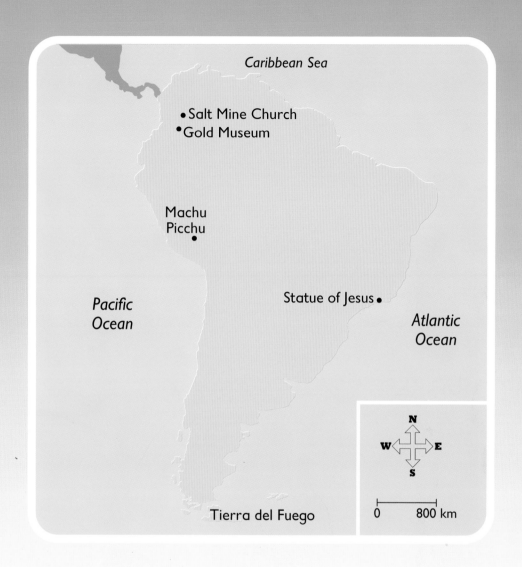

Caribbean Sea

• Salt Mine Church
• Gold Museum

Machu
Picchu

Statue of Jesus •

Pacific
Ocean

Atlantic
Ocean

N
W E
S

Tierra del Fuego

0   800 km

Tierra del Fuego is a group of rocky islands at the tip of
South America. Its name means 'Land of fire' in Spanish.
500 years ago, explorers saw camp fires on the islands and
gave them this name. Today Tierra del Fuego is a national
park. Penguins and seals swim around the islands' shores.

Fast Facts

1. South America has the world's largest rainforest – the Amazon rainforest. It covers an area bigger than France, Spain and Germany put together.

2. The Atacama Desert in northern Chile is one of the driest places in the world.

3. Angel Falls in Venezuela has a longer drop than any other waterfall in the world. The water falls for nearly one kilometre.

4. The city of Quito, in the mountains of Ecuador, is almost three kilometres above the Pacific Ocean.

5. South America has some of the largest farms in the world.

6. The hottest weather in South America is in Argentina's Gran Chaco, where the temperature reaches 43°C.

7. The Andes Mountains are the longest mountain range in the world. They stretch for over 7200 kilometres.

8. The Amazon rainforest has more kinds of plants than any other forest in the world.

9. The Amazon River is the second longest river in the world. It is 6400 kilometres long.

Glossary

ancestors family members who lived a long time ago

capital city city where government leaders work

dung droppings of large animals, such as horses or llamas

equator imaginary circle around the exact middle of the Earth

erupt to throw out rocks and hot ash

export to send goods to another country to be sold

festival a time when people celebrate something

gorge very deep river valley with steep, rocky sides

herder someone who looks after a group of animals

humid warm and damp

malaria disease causing fevers

mine to dig up things from under the Earth's surface

mouth place where a river meets the sea

national park area of wild land protected by the government

Native Americans first people to live in South America

observatory building where people study the stars

rainforest thick forest that has heavy rain all the year round

range line of connected mountains

sap liquid from a plant or tree

settlers people who come to live in a country

source place where a river begins

timber cut up wood used for making things

tropical hot and wet

volcano hole in the earth from which hot, melted rock is thrown out

More books to read

An Illustrated Atlas of South America, Keith Lye,
Cherrytree Books,1999

South America, Mike Graf, Bridgestone
Books, 2002

Index